LEARNING POWER
HEROES

A Scrapbook of Ideas by
Raegan Delaney, Leanne Day and Maryl Chambers

Published in 2009 by TLO Limited
Henleaze House, Harbury Road, Bristol BS9 4PN

ISBN 978 1 901219 53 1

We are built to learn by imitation. Evolution has equipped us with brains that are designed from the moment of birth to do what people around us are doing. When a baby sees you make a fist or a smile the neurons in her brain make her ready to do the same thing.

It's through this kind of unconscious osmosis that children learn the habits of language and culture into which they have been born. Without any instruction from us, their brains start moulding themselves to the social world around them. They pick up the speech sounds and accents they hear and the emotional reactions they see being modelled. By watching us they learn to be frightened of what we are frightened of, to ignore what we ignore, to find funny what we laugh at.

And in just the same way they learn to learn in the way their parents, carers and teachers learn. If they grow up around people who

love to debate round the dinner table they will imbibe the habits, rules and pleasures of debating. If they watch adults being experimental, inquisitive and tenacious in their learning these habits will rub off too. If their role models have no time for ideas, or become angry the minute their efforts are frustrated, that too is what they will learn.

So we must be careful to be at our learning best around young children, especially if they like or admire us, for their 'heroes' are the people whose habits they will find most contagious. Capitalising on this rubbing-off of learning habits gives us a powerful way of influencing children's development — for good or ill.

It is not just us: learning heroes (and heroines) come in all shapes and sizes. Celebrities like David Beckham can be heroes not just because they are handsome and successful

but because they overcome set-backs and put in the hard hours of practice. Characters like Gandalf, or even Tinky-Winky, can impress with their tenacity or thoughtfulness. A child's grandmother can be a source of inspiration through her ability to invite calm discussion of a vexed issue in a stressed family. Children can be helped to see admirable characteristics in their playmates. And most importantly of all, every child can be their own Learning Hero, as they feed off the memories of their own resilience and resourcefulness.

This book shows how primary schools are capitalising on children's powers of imitation, to help them build strong foundations for their own learning lives. I hope you will find much to admire and to imitate in these pages.

Guy Claxton

Professor Guy Claxton is programme consultant, and chief inspiration, for TLO's Building Learning Power programme

BUILDING LEARNING POWER

WHAT IS BLP?

A Practical Framework

Over the last five years or so, schools across the UK have been introduced to an approach to learning-to-learn known as Building Learning Power. Many schools are now putting that approach into practice. This eminently practical framework of learning dispositions and capacities (see opposite) was researched and put together by Professor Guy Claxton. It offers teachers a real opportunity to help all their students to become confident, capable, creative lifelong learners.

A Good Learner

The Learning Power framework provides a clear picture of what it takes to be a good learner. The purpose of the approach is to grow students' learning character and habits. In so doing, Building Learning Power (BLP) develops the appetite and ability to learn in different ways, and shifts the responsibility for learning to learn from the teacher to the learner.

A Transforming Culture

Making learning power work often involves transforming the culture of the classroom and the climate of the school. A common language for learning is adopted across the whole school; staff model learning themselves by sharing their own difficulties, frustrations and triumphs in learning; students come to understand themselves as growing learners and consciously improve their learning habits; teachers assume the role of learning-power coach, offering students interesting, real and challenging activities to enable them to create their own knowledge and stretch their learning habits.

A Creative Approach

The BLP approach does not aim to provide teachers with neat boxes of resources that can be assembled into set lessons. Headteachers and staff are encouraged to work creatively with the principles and examples of practice in order to grow and personalise the approach for their own students.

The following pages reveal creative and practical examples of some ways in which four schools have done this: growing and stimulating students' understanding of learning, stimulating enthusiasm for learning, transforming teaching, and building students' lifelong learning habits.

Be ready to be inspired!

THE LEARNING POWER FRAMEWORK

THE LEARNING POWER DISPOSITIONS

Emotional Engagement	Cognitive Range	Interpersonal Involvement	Strategic Responsibility
RESILIENCE	**RESOURCEFULNESS**	**RECIPROCITY**	**REFLECTIVENESS**
Feeling, Attending	Thinking	Relating	Managing

THE LEARNING POWER CAPACITIES

Absorption
Being able to lose yourself in learning — becoming absorbed in what you are doing; rapt and attentive, in a state of 'flow'.

Managing Distractions
Recognising and reducing distractions; knowing when to walk away and refresh yourself. Creating your own best environment for learning.

Noticing
Perceiving subtle nuances, patterns and details in experience.

Perseverance
Keeping going in the face of difficulties, channelling the energy of frustration productively. Knowing what a slow and uncertain process learning often is.

Questioning
Asking questions of yourself and others. Being curious and playful with ideas — delving beneath the surface of things.

Making Links
Seeing connections between disparate events and experiences — building patterns — weaving a web of understanding.

Imagining
Using your imagination and intuition to put yourself through new experiences or to explore possibilities. Wondering What if ...?

Reasoning
Calling up your logical and rational skills to work things out methodically and rigorously; constructing good arguments, and spotting the flaws in others'.

Capitalising
Drawing on the full range of resources from the wider world — other people, books, the Internet, past experience, future opportunities ...

Interdependence
Knowing when it's appropriate to learn on your own or with others, and being able to stand your ground in debate.

Collaboration
Knowing how to manage yourself in the give and take of a collaborative venture, respecting and recognising other viewpoints; adding to and drawing from the strength of teams.

Empathy and Listening
Contributing to others' experiences by listening to them to understand what they are really saying, and putting yourself in their shoes.

Imitation
Constructively adopting methods, habits or values from other people whom you observe.

Planning
Thinking about where you are going, the action you are going to take, the time and resources you will need, and the obstacles you may encounter.

Revising
Being flexible, changing your plans in the light of different circumstances, monitoring and reviewing how things are going and seeing new opportunities.

Distilling
Looking at what is being learned — pulling out the essential features — carrying them forward to aid further learning; being your own learning coach.

Meta-learning
Knowing yourself as a learner — how you learn best; how to talk about the learning process.

ABOUT THE AUTHORS

RAEGAN DELANEY

LEANNE DAY

Raegan has contributed numerous examples of practice from her own school.

Leanne has contributed a range of examples of practice from schools she has worked with in Kent.

I have been involved in primary education for twenty-two years in this country and overseas as a teacher, a school leader, a consultant partner and most recently a SIP. I am passionate about children's learning and committed to sharing this with children, other teachers and school leaders.

I have been head teacher of Nayland County Primary School since September 1999. Nayland was a good school when I was appointed and the challenge of taking an already successful school to new heights has been a delicate process. A cultural change that embraces risk-taking for teachers as well as pupils has been a key feature of improvement. In September 2005 OFSTED considered Nayland an outstanding school, describing leadership as 'outstanding … outward looking and eager to get involved with any new initiatives that have something important to offer the pupils.'

'Building Learning Power' has offered all of our children the opportunity to take charge of their own learning and to have fun developing the skills that will keep them learning for life. The balance between the 'what' and the 'how' of learning has enabled every child, regardless of age or abilities, to feel empowered and grow in confidence, motivation, self-esteem and power!

Maryl Chambers

Maryl Chambers has spearheaded the development of TLO Limited's Building Learning Power programme, helping bring Guy Claxton's ground-breaking work to schools and teachers. Maryl is one of the founders of TLO, where she has applied her wide experience of designing learning-focused training to creating and developing the innovative programmes for which the company is renowned. She is co-author of many of TLO's publications.

I began my teaching career in Liverpool where I taught for eleven years, spending eight years as Deputy Headteacher at St. John's C of E Primary School in Sefton. In 2005 I joined Kent's Advisory Service as a centrally based Advanced Skills Teacher. In this role I worked in partnership with teachers to develop creative approaches to teaching and learning; a major part of this being the implementation of Building Learning Power. I supported teachers, through modelling and coaching, in actively developing BLP in their classrooms. I went on to lead on the development of BLP, providing support to Advisory Service Teams, School Leadership Teams and teachers through the development of county-wide learning networks and a series of county conferences.

For me BLP has brought a new dimension to teaching and learning. Making learning to learn really explicit seems so obvious now and something I really couldn't teach without. BLP enables children to find ways for themselves, it gives them confidence to have a go and increases independence. Seeing children take great strides in their learning and being able to explain clearly how they got there is extremely rewarding.

Nayland Primary School

Nayland County Primary School Suffolk is a semi-rural first school on the Suffolk–Essex border, catering for 145 children from nursery to Year 4. The school population is quite diverse but with a low percentage of children entitled to FSMs and below average special needs. Children enter the Foundation Stage broadly in line with national abilities but attainment at KS1 and Year 4 milestones are significantly above national expectations.

The staff pride themselves on their willingness to keep learning about learning. They have established an action research culture as part of this commitment to their learning partnership with 10 other local schools. The school bumped into BLP when the head teacher chanced to meet teachers from schools in Bath at an NCSL event, and returned totally fired up.

The learning partnership, HELP (Helping Effective Learning Partnerships), sent out a search party to visit these schools in Bath

and hear from the children whether Building Learning Power was all it was cracked up to be. As well as the obvious benefits to the learners, BLP has sharpened the teachers' focus and helped them to ensure they consider the impact of everything they do in school in terms of how it moves learning forward.

Christ Church C of E Primary School

Christ Church is a two-form entry Primary School with 420 children on roll, situated near the centre of Folkestone. The eastern part of Folkestone is considered an area of high social deprivation, and 95% of the pupils come from this area, with 31% of pupils eligible for FSM.

The Headteacher trained as a BLP trainer in 2005. Since then he has been committed to ensuring that all teaching and support staff are trained in and understand the importance of BLP and how to use it. A rolling programme of training has allowed time to develop ideas and ensure consistency. This has enabled newly trained members of the team to see BLP in action and deepen their understanding.

Year 6 teachers began exploring the use of learning heroes in September 2007. The impact on the children has been tremendous and they have now begun to extend this learning throughout the school.

In this unique book, four schools share the development of learning power through the use of learning heroes. The schools are on an exciting, never-ending, learning journey and have been kind enough to share their ideas so far.

Ashford South Primary School, Ashford, Kent

Ashford South Primary School has 250 children on roll and serves an area of high social deprivation. The proportion of pupils eligible for free school meals is higher than average, as is the proportion with learning difficulties or disabilities. Pupils come from a wide range of ethnic backgrounds and there has been a recent influx of EAL pupils. Attainment on entry to the school is lower than the national average.

Several teachers have attended a BLP Foundation Course and this ensured the approach became contagious. Conversations took place naturally in the staffroom, helping keep the momentum going.

Staff hold learning walks each term which involve walking around the school and sharing their learning environments. Each teacher talks about what they are doing and how. This 'in it together' approach has helped build everyone's confidence.

Staplehurst Primary School, Kent

Staplehurst Primary has 396 pupils on roll, who come from a wide range of social and economic backgrounds. Almost 90% are White British. The attainment of pupils on entry to the school is average, as is the proportion of pupils with learning difficulties. Their journey with BLP began in June 2005 when two teachers attended Kent's Creativity Conference where they were inspired by Professor Guy Claxton.

Teachers attended a BLP Foundation Course and began to drip feed ideas and coaching to other staff. The language of learning was slowly developed with the children which helped them to begin to talk about how they learn.

Further training took place and the approach was relaunched in the school in September 2007.

Learning Power Heroes

CONTENTS

SECTION: 1

CREATING A LEARNING CULTURE

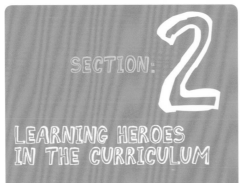

SECTION: 2

LEARNING HEROES IN THE CURRICULUM

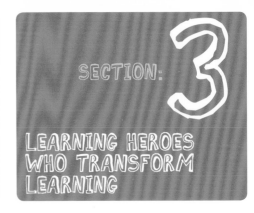

SECTION: 3

LEARNING HEROES WHO TRANSFORM LEARNING

CREATING A LEARNING CULTURE

In this section we meet the schools and hear about how they have used the idea of Learning Heroes to create a powerful learning culture in the school.

Firstly, we see how younger children have been introduced to their learning powers through the use of puppets, and how these imaginary learning heroes have influenced and enhanced pupils' engagement with learning.

Then there are examples of how schools have used famous people as learning heroes to good effect, and how children have been encouraged to see themselves as learning heroes.

Later examples show how a school celebrates learning-to-learn behaviours in assemblies and star books, and how, over time, such celebrations have moved in emphasis: from celebrating outcomes to celebrating learning behaviours.

We learn too about how schools are making good use of learning walls, scrapbooks and 'split page' books to help children reflect on and better understand themselves as learners.

And finally we are treated to lots of little ideas that have helped schools grow their learning-powered culture.

IMAGINARY LEARNING HEROES

MILAN REFLECTIVE

Milan is a real planner. Before starting a task he thinks carefully about what he needs to learn, any obstacles that may get in his way and what he needs to be successful. He is a flexible learner who asks himself questions about how well things are going, and he isn't afraid to change his plan when necessary. Milan can look back on his learning, tell everyone how he learned, and pick out the most important parts to use again. He watches other children carefully and helps them to be reflective too.

BILLY RESILIENT

Billy is not interested in an easy ride because he knows that this will not move his learning on. He likes to be challenged and is 'up for anything!' That doesn't mean that he is a brain box; he just sticks at his learning and tries a range of methods until he gets there. Sometimes he takes a break and comes back to a task later when his brain has had a rest. Billy can get absolutely lost in his learning and even his best buddy, the class clown, can't distract him because he has learned to block out things that could sidetrack him from his goal. He also has eagle eyes and notices everything!

SYLVIE RESOURCEFUL

Sylvie can't stop herself from asking questions. She wonders about everything so much that she's had to learn how to find answers from a wide range of sources. She loves to 'Google,' an encyclopaedia is a treasure to her, she watches TV to store up information and if she cannot find out for herself she is confident enough to ask others. She even asks her granny by text! Sylvie likes to imagine what the outcome might look like when she starts something so that she knows what she is working towards! She can take a step-by-step approach to learning, and link what she has learned before to new learning.

POLLY RECIPROCITY

Polly loves to learn with other people. She encourages everyone in her group to take on a role and get involved, but she can also see when it would be best to learn on her own. Polly likes to watch and listen to others and imitate their successes. But she isn't sneaky about it, she will congratulate her friends on their great ideas and ask if she can use them to help her. She can put herself in someone else's shoes and tries to feel how they feel, so her classmates love to work together with her.

USING IMAGINARY LEARNING HEROES
TO INTRODUCE LEARNING BEHAVIOURS TO YOUNG CHILDREN

WHERE WE STARTED

With our younger learners we wanted to find a way of referring to learning capacities that was more than a flat wall display: something that was fairly permanent, but could be moved; something that was interactive and that caught the children's interest. We found some discarded puppets, two boys and two girls — just what we needed!

WHAT WE DID

We introduced Polly Reciprocity, Milan Reflective, Sylvie Resourceful and Billy Resilient one at a time to the children and talked about the kinds of learning powers they each had. Teachers used the puppets to ask questions and make suggestions at the start of a learning activity, or comment on the children's learning and nudge them along.

The puppets have little bags containing suggestions and comments and stickers to give to the children when congratulating them. For example, Sylvie might give a 'Sylvie's Hero' sticker for asking great questions.

HOW IT DEVELOPED

The puppets were invited into assembly, and we were surprised by how much the older children identified with the puppets' learning powers. The older children asked for posters to remind them of the four characters and they talked about their own learning behaviours in terms of how they were like Polly, Milan, Sylvie and Billy. Later they wrote stories about the characters and made animations for the younger children.

IMPACT ON THE CHILDREN

Having an imaginary learning hero character to whom they could relate learning capacities helped the children to 'see' what these behaviours looked like. Thus Polly showed them how to be a good listener and how to look at something from another person's point of view.

The characters helped the children in a friendly way, rather like a super-peer role model: e.g. Billy encouraging a Nursery age boy not to give up on a rather tricky puzzle.

Nursery and Reception children now go and find the relevant puppet and tell them about their learning using amazing language!

We didn't expect the older children to take to the puppet characters; but they found the whole thing amusing and it has caused them to talk to the younger children about their learning and be supportive.

OVER TO YOU

- How might you use or adapt this idea for your own class?
- Do you have some old puppets lurking at the back of a cupboard?
- What sort of imaginary characters would your children take to?
- Which well-known imaginary characters act in these ways and would fit the bill?
- How would you introduce these characters to your children?
- Would you use the same characters in every class?
- Could older children suggest and vote for imaginary characters that would become the class's learning heroes?

IMAGINARY LEARNING HEROES

FATHER CHRISTMAS

The children chose Father Christmas as a learning hero in the week before Christmas. They had fun exploring how he was challenged in his job, ensuring all the presents were delivered on time. These are some examples of the children's evaluation of Father Christmas's learning power:

- **Capitalising:** Father Christmas capitalises on the elves' skills when deciding who should make different toys.

- **Planning:** Father Christmas plans really well; he decides what needs to be done, when and by whom. He draws a map of his route on Christmas Eve and records times to arrive at certain places.

- **Perseverance:** Father Christmas is very good at persevering; he makes sure he has a clear idea of what he should be doing and keeps on going until he finishes. He takes a break when he needs to and listens to music to help him concentrate.

- **Revising:** Father Christmas thinks about what he did last year to help him this year; he revises his route and reorganises the workshop.

SAM SATS

In the run up to SATs week the children developed their own imaginary learning hero Sam SATs. They talked about how he would behave in the SATs tests. For example he would:

- **Plan:** Sam plans his writing carefully, thinking about the genre in terms of structure and organisation and the effect on the reader.

  He also takes note of the time to help him make sure he has time to finish the test. He tries to answer every question, knowing a good guess might get him a mark.

- **Question:** Sam questions himself about which method to use to answer a Maths question.

- **Notice:** Sam notices how many marks a question is worth and uses this to help him decide how to answer it.

- **Persevere:** Sam keeps on going and doesn't give up.

- **Imitate:** Sam imitates his teacher and his classmates to help him revise previous learning and make sure he has a method he can use well.

CHARLIE BUCKET

Children attributed the following learning capacities to Charlie Bucket from *Charlie and the Chocolate Factory* by Roald Dahl:

- **Reasoning:** Charlie makes logical decisions about what's right and what's wrong to help him make the best choice. Charlie reasons with himself.

- **Questioning:** Charlie questions himself about how to get a golden ticket.

- **Imagining:** Charlie uses his imagination to create pictures in his head about what Willy Wonka's factory might look like.

- **Making Links:** Charlie makes links between the actions and behaviour of other children in the chocolate factory and the things that happen to them.

- **Capitalising:** Each year for his birthday Charlie is given a bar of chocolate, which he likes to make last. He makes best use of his resources, he capitalises on them.

USING IMAGINARY LEARNING HEROES TO DEVELOP AN UNDERSTANDING OF LEARNING POWER

WHERE WE STARTED

Our Year 6 children knew what building learning power was and could name the four R's. However, their knowledge and understanding of the learning capacities was superficial. We hoped that using learning heroes as a stimulus would motivate and enthuse the children, help them to explore the learning capacities and develop strategies of their own.

WHAT WE DID

Initially children collected pictures and examples of their heroes. Having evaluated learning, the teachers decided to focus on developing the children's resourcefulness and began to discuss how their heroes were resourceful. Teachers modelled examples and encouraged children to add their own ideas to a class learning wall.

Alongside this, 'warming up for learning' sessions were introduced first thing in the morning to allow children to explore learning capacities and build success criteria for them. Teachers draw on this throughout the day.

HOW IT DEVELOPED

Learning heroes are now changed fortnightly in consultation with the children. The children thought it would be a good idea to use heroes for different projects they are studying so, for example, Jenner was a learning hero when the children were learning about micro-organisms.

A class book of learning heroes is being developed which holds all the heroes explored together with the children's comments about them.

IMPACT ON THE CHILDREN

Children now talk about learning and are really excited about learning rather than doing. Involving the children in the decision-making process of selecting the hero has shown them that their ideas and opinions are valued. The children have the language to talk about learning and draw on past and present learning heroes frequently.

A warm-up activity:
Using imagination

Remember to:
- Look carefully at the objects
- Think about what they might be used for
- Think beyond the obvious
- Make creative suggestions

Provide the children with a range of objects. What might they be used for? Encourage the children to think of as many uses as possible, beyond the obvious. Introduce one at a time, what can we do if we use more than one at a time?

Discuss what the children did to be imaginative. Generate strategies.

OVER TO YOU

- How might you use or adapt this wider use of learning heroes?
- Might this idea help your pupils to better understand the learning capacities?
- Would changing the learning heroes fortnightly work for your class?
- Are you aware of which learning capacities your pupils need to work on most?
- How might you find out if not?
- Find more ideas for using learning heroes in literacy, science and maths in Section 2.
- Find out more about learning warm-ups on page 25.

FAMOUS LEARNING HEROES

"I made links between World War I and World War II"

"I wanted to find out about the enemy so I would know where to send the army. I listened to all of the arguments and suggestions before making a decision. I used reasoning skills."

"I asked women to work in the factories while the men were away fighting. I capitalised on resources."

"I capitalised on my resources and used rationing to share all of the food and clothing fairly."

"I used my imagination to picture how it would feel and what it would be like to win the war. It helped me to know what strategies to use."

"I made links between all of the information about Nazis and used to it plan ahead."

"I used my imagination when I wondered what would happen if we lost the war. It made me work hard to win!"

"I always asked lots of questions. This was helpful to gather opinions and ideas, I had to find the best way forward and learn from previous mistakes."

WHERE WE STARTED

The children chose Winston Churchill as their learning hero when they were learning about World War II. They were inspired by his resourcefulness; and how he responded to the needs of the country by capitalising on the limited resources available to him.

WHAT WE DID

We used role play to explore a range of situations; for example, the children had conversations about how best to ensure children in cities were kept safe. They considered how these children may have felt and the impact this would have on family life. This deepened their understanding of empathy and listening skills. The children thought about what Churchill might have done and how he would have capitalised on the skills and experience of others by effective questioning, making links between information they provided and his own experience. They thought that Churchill would have made pictures in his mind's eye, imagining the effect of his decisions on the families and children. They also felt that he would need time for evaluation and reflection because he was having to make such important decisions. The girls were interested in Churchill's decisions about women in the war and how they too were learning heroes since they had to learn completely new jobs to support their communities.

EXPLORING THE DEEDS OF FAMOUS PEOPLE THROUGH THE FRAMEWORK OF LEARNING POWER

HOW IT DEVELOPED

The children empathised with Churchill by imagining the enormity of the challenges he faced. He seemed to appear in every aspect of our learning! The children referred to his learning strategies and skills to help them understand how the situations of World War II were managed.

Winston Churchill led us to explore other learning heroes related to World War II. The children were inspired by Admiral Ramsay after visiting the tunnels at Dover, and spent time at home as well as in school finding out about him.

IMPACT ON THE CHILDREN

The children's enthusiasm for learning grew and grew. Seeing things from someone else's perspective enabled them to develop real understanding of what it means to use your imagination. They generated a range of strategies for learning which they have carried through into all aspects of school life and at home.

For example, through active discussion and exploration using warm-ups and then a series of history-based enquiries, the children began to imitate some of the strategies Churchill used. They read and analysed evidence to make informed decisions in response to questions and challenges. They used their imagination to create new scenarios in response to given actions and ideas.

The children's language changed; they now talk confidently about the 'how' as well as the 'what' when learning.

NELSON MANDELA

One class were discussing bullying as a class, using SEAL materials, and this led to talk about racism, apartheid and Nelson Mandela. The children asked if they could have him as their learning hero in order to learn more about him and the things he had done. They researched him for home learning and produced PowerPoint presentations about his life, what he had done and how.

"Nelson Mandela collaborated with others when he tried to stop apartheid. He imagined what the world would be like if it didn't exist and used this to help people understand what needed to change. He planned what he could do to help it to stop. He listened to people and empathised with them to understand how things needed to develop. He was interdependent. Nelson Mandela persevered even when he was threatened and attacked. He noticed how apartheid affected people's lives."

Jessica, Y6 Christ Church C of E Primary School.

OVER TO YOU

- How might you use famous people as learning heroes?

- Who would your children choose as their learning hero?

- How would you blend the deeds of famous people with their learning-power capacities?

- You might use historical figures, scientists, artists, politicians or sports people.

- How might you extend the idea of famous learning heroes into writing, maths or science activities?

FAMILY LEARNING HEROES

My • Learn

"My brother's my learning hero because he always perseveres with his homework. He makes links between things he's done in school and at home. He's absorbed in what he does and notices how others are feeling. He's helped me by being a good role model. He helps me to be absorbed and to persevere; he sits down and goes through things with me, showing me different ways and giving me examples."

Katie, Y6

"My sister's my learning hero. If I have homework she helps me, she's focused and doesn't leave it to the last minute; she manages her distractions well. She empathises with me; she knows how it feels to have to do homework when you really want to play outside! She perseveres and notices small details. This helps me to collaborate with others because I can imitate what my sister does."

Jaimie, Y6

"My Mum's my learning hero. She encourages me when I have homework and helps me out. She notices when I'm sad and upset and when I'm doing good and bad things. She helps me capitalise on using the computer. She always plans her day before she starts."

Hayden, Y6

Year 5

ng • hero! s

WHERE WE STARTED

Our earlier work on famous learning-power heroes had been so successful that we wanted to use the ideas to bring learning power into the everyday lives of the children.

WHAT WE DID

We invited our children to think about people in their families they particularly admire, and asked them about what these people did and how. Initially the children's responses were linked to everyday actions, but as the questions continued and we kept saying 'But how..?' the responses became more insightful.

IMPACT ON THE CHILDREN

Through these explorations the children began to look at people in their everyday lives differently. They began to recognise and value how people do things and began to take more notice of what people did that might help them with their own learning. Family heroes have become more prominent in our discussions and the children more readily refer to their family heroes, giving examples of things they have noticed.

My mum is my learning hero because she uses so many BLP skills.

She perserveres [sic] in all she does and never gives up no matter how tough the challenge may be.

She is always absorped [sic] in her cooking and creates new and delicious recipes.

My mum always notices when me or my little brother are doing something we should not be doing.

When my mum is faced with a challenge she is resourceful because she uses what is available to make that challenge easier.

If my mum didn't plan holidays and partys [sic] ahead my family would all be in chaos.

She cheers me up when I am feeling blue because I know that inside she really loves and cares about me even when she tells me off for no reason at all.

Year 6

OVER TO YOU

- Where might you fit family learning heroes into your curriculum?

- What questions would help your children to explore family members as learning heroes?

- Could you extend this idea to learning heroes in everyday life, e.g. people outside their family they know and admire, and whose learning habits they could imitate?

- How might you extend these explorations into writing, speaking and listening, and reading activities?

- Which storybook characters would lend themselves to initiating discussions of everyday learning heroes?

PUPILS AS LEARNING HEROES

WHERE WE STARTED

Most children love superheroes, be it Spiderman, Elastigirl or Jedi Knights. They see these characters as powerful and in control. We wanted to help children to see themselves as powerful and in charge of their own learning, and thought the superhero theme might work. We encouraged the children to see their learning strengths as super-powers that would help them to be learning heroes in many situations both in and out of school.

SUPERHERO COSTUMES

Every child designed a superhero costume for themselves. Some were quite traditional and others ended up with super high heels and super pets. We took a photograph of each child's face and added this to their costume. The outcomes were very amusing. During this design process the children had to be thinking of a facet of learning that was a personal strength, together with an example of when they had used that learning skill very well. We encouraged them to consider their learning in school and in out-of-school situations. One Year 4 boy focused on his ability to manage distractions when riding motocross and how this had enabled him to win a championship! We used the pictures and comments to create a whole-school display showing that everyone has a super-learning strength. The children also gave their class a hero group name and so The Outstanding Owls and The Wonderful Woodpeckers were created.

DRESSING UP DAYS

The children enjoyed this so much we though we might go a step further. We arranged a special day when the children came to school dressed in their learning superhero costume. Some tried very hard to create their designed costume for real while others just wore their pants over their trousers! All the children wore a sign or a badge telling of their super-power. The day was focused on recognising that everyone has learning power and can use this power to help others with their learning too. It was a hilarious event; learning should include laughter.

CHILDREN UNDERSTANDING THEMSELVES AS LEARNING HEROES

Imagining: In Imagin when I'm upset I'm in a calm spacegoul place.

Macking Links: When I'm stack on my task I think if there is any think I have done to help me.

Questioning: I question what the task is so know what I'm doing.

Colaboration: I Colaborat with people I'm not been on.

Ashford South Primary School

✓ I am a learning superhero because I like a challenge. I am learning to ride my bike without stabilisers.
Emily, Y1 Nayland School

✓ I am a learning superhero because I am very good at asking questions. I want to find out!
Ethan, Y2 Nayland School

✓ My super learning power is imagination because I use it in my stories and they turn out really well. So work harder on your imagination and you will be able to write perfect stories.
Nia, Y4 Nayland School

✓ My super learning power is collaborating because I work as part of a team and I listen to others and they listen to me. I collaborated in maths with my friend because he didn't understand.
Alex, Y4 Nayland School

LINKS TO SEAL

We use the idea of learning heroes to link to a range of topic areas. Younger children in thinking about 'people who help us' through PSE or SEAL design themselves a uniform and comment on the learning powers they need in their job. Future dressing-up days will be around these helpful people, and the school will invite 'real people who help us' to be interviewed by their emulators. We will need to let the visitors know that they will be asked what learning powers they have! This work has helped us to anchor learning power in real life, even with Foundation Stage children.

OVER TO YOU

- What learning powers could your children claim right now?

- It might be fun to guess which learning powers each child thinks they have before they draw their character.

- How about a dressing-up day in your school involving everyone?

- If finding entire costumes is a bit too much, could children carry a big badge with a hero picture or an appropriate artifact instead?

- Could they interview each other to try and discover who they represent and which learning skill they consider as their strength(s)?

- How might you link these ideas to literacy, history, geography, science, music etc.?

LEARNING-POWER ASSEMBLIES

WHAT WE DO NOW

During the week a class of children may be focusing on particular capacities linked to their topic area, e.g. planning and imagination in DT, or capitalising in geography. Another class may have been concentrating on building power in an area of learning weakness, e.g. a class who are poor collaborators, or who struggle to listen and be empathetic. Weekly celebration assemblies are an opportunity to bring the whole school back to the big picture of learning.

A display that can accommodate all the learning capacities for all of the classes in the school can be used as a great motivator. At the moment we use a simple landscape display with lots of sky and a set of balloons and kites. Each class is given the opportunity to suggest how they have strengthened certain learning capacities and then their kite rises up into the sky. The children can get quite carried away with 'higher, higher' demands, and while this is hardly a scientific estimate of their progress, their enthusiasm for learning can't be questioned!

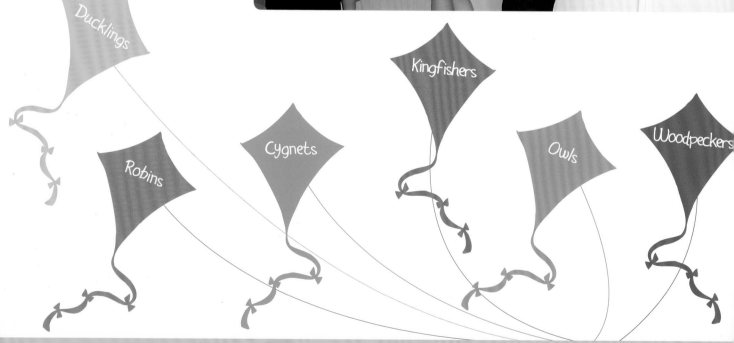

AND STAR BOOKS

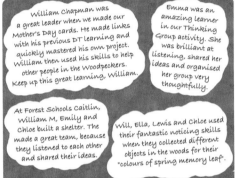

William Chapman was a great leader when we made our Mother's Day cards. He made links with his previous DT learning and quickly mastered his own project. William then used his skills to help other people in the Woodpeckers. Keep up this great learning, William.

Emma was an amazing learner in our Thinking Group activity. She was brilliant at listening, shared her ideas and organised her group very thoughtfully.

At Forest Schools Caitlin, William M, Emily and Chloe built a shelter. The made a great team, because they listened to each other and shared their ideas.

Will, Ella, Lewis and Chloe used their fantastic noticing skills when they collected different objects in the woods for their "colours of spring memory leaf".

Bobbie, Kye, Abigail and Rosie M have been great powerful learners. They showed great resilience and persevered to complete these challenging jigsaw puzzles.

Abigail showed she was a reciprocal learner and knew she could ask Rosie to help her.

HOW IT STARTED

One of the greatest motivators is a bit of success and we have always had a culture of celebrating in our school. A couple of years ago we asked the children about our traditional award system and were presented with a few home truths.

"We know you give everyone a turn at getting the class award, I could get it every week but you save me for a week when one of the naughty children hasn't been good."

"What if a whole group of children deserve an award, why do you have to choose one?"

"The 'art cup' is unfair because when some people are born they can do art and they just keep getting better but other children are never good at art no matter how hard they try."

HOW IT DEVELOPED

We listened and changed our celebration assembly so that the children decide weekly on the criteria for the class awards and vote for the recipient. Now, if someone deserves it two weeks running they get it! We also introduced 'Star Books' and celebrated any number of super-learning outcomes every week at each child's best level.

However, recently, with no staff meeting or pupil consultation we have seen a shift. Gradually children began setting criteria for one another that centred on the 'how' of learning as well as being a good school citizen. 'Star Books' are now populated with celebrations of the process of learning with hardly an outcome in sight. This shift was so natural within our new school ethos of balancing learning skills with content that we didn't really notice until we looked back at two-year-old 'Star Books.' The difference was incredible; we now have a school full of 'how to learn' heroes.

OVER TO YOU

- What kinds of things do you celebrate in assemblies or class books?

- How might you use assemblies to bring ideas of learning power together?

- Who decides the criteria for class or individual awards? Could you hand this over to the children?

- What do you think would happen in the school if you started to celebrate learning qualities as well as outcomes?

BOASTER POSTERS AND OTHER CELEBRATION IDEAS

BOASTER POSTER BOARD

The whole school community is learning all of the time and yet our national culture of reservation doesn't encourage us to brag. We wanted to break that culture and started a 'Boaster Poster' board to encourage our learning community to blow their own trumpets! We use the board to display a whole range of awards, accomplishments, good deeds and so on, from both home and school life. We make sure it is not just about the children; grown-ups should flaunt their learning too.

When the Reception Class wrote a letter to a magazine and received a reply and some model dinosaurs, they were so proud they stuck the dinosaurs up on the board — only temporarily! Our sports teams have had some wonderful successes this year and are celebrated alongside Freddie in Year 4 who is an amazing and dedicated motocross rider. The school choir have taken part in two local festivals and sung at many community events; they are boasting neighbours with their teacher who has completed the first part of her Kodaly training, and one of our treasured TAs who has just been awarded her Diploma in English Language Studies on her way to a degree.

We are hoping to encourage parents to join in soon.

ADMIRATION CARDS

We use a set of folded tags detailing learning dispositions like greetings cards for assessment for learning. We place them in a child's space during a learning task with a murmured or public positive comment; 'The way you made links with last week's learning on multiplication must have been really helpful. Well done.' We collect the cards at the end of the lesson ready to use again.

SPEAK OUT

When a teacher models 'learning hero talk' the children soon join in.

'I am so proud of Phoebe, she is my learning hero this morning. When that very big puzzle got too tricky she asked her friends to help her. She knows when to learn on her own and when to collaborate with others. What a powerful learner!'

Give it a week, you know those little foundation and KS1 sponges will be imitating your every word.

5H Star of the Week...

JOSH!

- He's great at football, swimming and basket ball - a fast, fast runner!
- He's a good mate with wicked hair.
- He's weird but in a good way.
- He has good noticing skills.
- He's funny - a real cool dude.
- He is top banana and a cheeky monkey.
- He is getting better at managing his distractions.
- He's a good learner and we're glad to have him in our class!

Dear Thomas,
You are such a brilliant imitator! Well learned,
Miss Delaney

LEARNATIC STICKERS

We encourage children to show one another and others outside of school just how proud they are to be 'into' learning. Our 'Proud to be a learnatic' stickers are a fun way of recognising their efforts, but they also get parents asking what it is all about when they wear them home with pride. You could ask your children to come up with their own fun phrase for 'into learning' stickers.

LEARNING HERO OF THE WEEK

We use circle time to discuss our learning each week and to positively identify children who have done well. Initially the children who were seen as being traditionally successful were selected; good students as opposed to good learners. However, as discussion gradually changed through modelling from the teacher, the children began to realise that just because someone didn't get it 'right' didn't mean they weren't a good learner. We talked about Karl who had really persevered with his learning in a science investigation by repeating the test when it had gone wrong. We also thought about Sophie who had imitated the process her friend had used to solve a Maths problem, showing that copying how it had been done was fine.

The children now value how they learn and are beginning to take greater notice of how others learn too.

LETTERS FROM TEACHERS

Our teachers write to learners on celebratory paper to congratulate them on their learning. Imagine arriving at school to find a note from last year's teacher attached to your recorded learning, congratulating you on how far you have come!

A sheet of 'special' paper that is instantly recognisable is all you need. Write a letter to a child when you notice impressive learning. You could leave it in their tray, send it home by post, attach it to their recorded learning on a display; whatever suits you and the child.

EXPLORING PERSEVERANCE

HOW IT DEVELOPED

The children came up with other situations where perseverance is important and drew their own split-page books. These included bike riding, and swimming where the 'give up' option showed a picture of a child in trouble in the water. In other lessons they explored more learning choices: e.g. to plan or not to plan, to adapt plans or leave them alone.

IMPACT ON THE CHILDREN

The children really began to explore how learning makes you feel and interestingly pointed out how making the easy (and wrong) choice can make you feel better in the short term.

They also explored the idea of taking a break, not persevering initially but leaving something and coming back to it. The teacher hadn't thought of this option and so let the children know that she had learned something unexpected.

They thoroughly enjoyed the humour of some of the scenarios and began to think of more and more ridiculous choices and outcomes. But they were using learning language throughout and recognising that they could make decisions and be in charge of their own learning. They were also keen to share and display their learning outcomes with other children

WHERE WE STARTED

Persevering with something is an important habit to establish early. We wanted our children to appreciate the potential impact their choices about persevering could have on their short- and long-term learning. We started in Year 2, showing them a picture of a girl holding a skipping rope. We didn't tell the children anything else as we wanted to work from their perceptions. We asked them to act as heroes, helping the girl with her learning.

WHAT WE DID

We asked the children what was happening in the picture and they thought the girl was having trouble learning to skip. We discussed how she might be feeling and what she might do. The children said she could persevere or give up and we wrote these two options on the opposite page that was split into two. The children shared how these two options might make the girl feel and what the consequences of each might be. We then revealed pictures; one of a happy girl skipping with her friends and one of a sad girl watching her friends skipping.

OVER TO YOU

- How might you tackle learning choices?

- What learning choices would suit your class?

- For example, sticking with playing the guitar could lead to being in a band, giving up leads to being in the audience!

- Pictures are a good starting point for learning choice stories.

- Try it using large sheets of paper as we did, or use ICT on an interactive whiteboard.

USING INTERACTIVE LEARNING WALLS

Part of a 'Learning Wall'.

WHERE WE STARTED

Literacy and numeracy working walls had been used previously to model learning processes and had been successful in moving learning on. We wanted to use some of the same ideas to help the children understand and relate to learning-power ideas.

WHAT WE DID

Initially we used a large display board to introduce the children to the idea of a learning hero and to model how heroes could be used, why, and in which contexts. We focused on one disposition (R) initially and discussed the learning capacities that make it up. The footballer Michael Owen was chosen as a resourceful learner because he is always asking himself questions about the best way to approach a game. These ideas were added to the wall using Post-it® notes, splats and speech bubbles. We kept blank copies next to the wall so the children could add to and amend ideas. They soon began to do so.

HOW IT DEVELOPED

The children quickly grasped the idea and began to think about the hero in wider contexts. They then considered all the other learning behaviours and identified those the hero might use most. This raised awareness of meta-learning, encouraging the children to really think about themselves as learners and to identify learning muscles they might need to practise flexing more often.

Our learning walls have now become more complex. The hero in focus is still prominent and children consider them in relation to all the learning behaviours. We used a set of picture symbols (an idea borrowed from another school); this has helped the children to recognise and remember the learning powers quickly. We also use learning warm-ups (see page 13). These are short learning episodes that allow the children to play with ideas and practise using a specific learning behaviour.

For example, we showed a range of pictures on the interactive whiteboard and asked the children to make as many links as possible between them. The children identified numerous links; obvious, imaginary, obscure and absurd. They then questioned each other about how they got there. Their link-making strategies were gathered, added to the learning wall, and thought about for learning across the curriculum; which strategies would be useful when, and why?

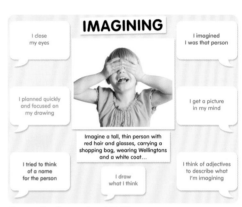

Part of a 'Learning Wall'.

We now use the picture symbols on all our learning walls to identify when we are using learning behaviours. Splats and speech bubbles are added by the children to explain how they have been used and the impact this has on their learning.

LEARNING-POWER TOOLS

WHERE WE STARTED

Our younger learners need physical prompts for many invisible concepts including learning. Since tools are what we use to help out with many jobs, we thought a set of learning tools might help children to connect with the idea of learning powers in a more tangible way.

WHAT WE DID

We bought real toolboxes from a DIY shop and set about gathering items to represent the seventeen learning capacities. Some of the items are obvious, like a blindfold for managing distractions and a magnifying glass for noticing details. Others are completely random like a plastic hammer for perseverance. For the more difficult ones we simply resorted to laminated clip art pictures, like a group of 'screen beans' carrying a giant key for collaboration.

We introduced the items to the children one at a time as the capacity represented fitted the learning content of the session. After a while we asked the children questions like 'Which learning tools will we need to help us today?' They were soon able to go and fetch the notebook that represented planning before they went outdoors to build a rocket, or the mirror of imitation if they were going to learn by watching someone else first.

Imitation

Can you learn from others by adopting methods, habits or values from other people you observe?

HOW IT DEVELOPED

Our Reception class children became more and more independent, getting a tool for themselves as appropriate and indeed offering the hammer of perseverance to an adult helper when she was struggling a little!

Year 1 liked the toolbox so much they got a replica! Finding the same tools was a bit of a nightmare so beware of your choices if you decide to make more than one!

A colleague from another school liked the idea so much that she imitated it, but using a set of icons to match the tools in the toolboxes. These icons have been used throughout the school, giving a sense of consistency and continuity

The icons are used in lesson openings when children are considering the learning powers they will need to stretch in the lesson. They are printed on the greeting cards that teachers use to commentate on and nudge the learning traits along. They are displayed around the school and used as an integral part of children evaluating their own learning. They have proved to be a valuable support to less able readers in accessing and using the learning language.

Reasoning

Do you use your logical skills to work things through step by step and carefully?

OVER TO YOU

- What icons for learning-power capacities would your children respond to?

- Would you want to stick to one set of icons for the whole school or use a different set for each class or year group?

- Could your older learners design a set of their own that could be used throughout the school?

- Clip art has proved a valuable place to look for ideas.

USING LEARNING-POWER SCRAPBOOKS

Show off
~~last years~~ I wanted to be able to:
Pass my 1st class in ballet
But I couldn't because:
I got just one step wrong.

My goal was to:
Pass my first ballet class.
Now I : can do my basic ballet.
because........
Step 1 I persevered, by practising at home every night and everyday.

INDIVIDUAL SCRAPBOOK

Children were encouraged to think about themselves as learners in all contexts — inside and outside of school time. This child has reflected on her ballet skills and how she had used her learning power to help her improve.

INDIVIDUAL SCRAPBOOK

Warm-ups (see page 13) are often used to delve deeper into learning behaviours and how to use them. These can be practical activities, investigations, drama or indeed written challenges. The children often choose to use strategies generated or ideas presented from these in their scrapbooks. They find them useful as prompts or to highlight unexpected outcomes.

CLASS SCRAPBOOK

All our heroes become part of our class scrapbook. The children go back to the heroes and think about how they might do something, particularly when they are stuck with their own learning.

WHERE WE STARTED

We wanted to find an exciting, child-led way for children to reflect on their learning skills and those of others. We introduced learning scrapbooks in which the children recorded their thoughts and strategies for learning, which they could refer back to at any time. The learning scrapbooks are more than a journal; we encourage children to make notes and share ideas in the best way for them.

WHAT WE DID

We had spent some time getting to grips with being a resourceful learner. The children were encouraged to reflect on this using the heroes we had explored and then to record, in their scrapbook, what they felt were the most important features of being a resourceful learner. They were given complete freedom about how they would record, but were encouraged to make use of text, diagrams, pictures and examples of resourcefulness in action. One child chose to present her learning as a table split into the five learning capacities. Under each capacity she made notes and drew pictures to explain how, for example, she had used her imagination. Another child used subheadings to identify each learning capacity, under which he recorded the strategies for making links together with examples of when he had used them and when they had been used by a hero. Some children wrote a great deal, others needed support to get started and suggestions for possible layouts and what they felt was important.

HOW IT DEVELOPED

The children now use their scrapbooks at least once a week. Sometimes this is teacher directed and follows on from learning where particular learning behaviours have been explored. At other times the children take the lead, taking their scrapbooks out and adding notes and ideas in lesson plenaries or in Golden Time. Some children have added a notes section at the back as an ongoing record that they refer to when they need to remind themselves of good learning strategies.

IMPACT ON THE CHILDREN

The children love the learning scrapbooks and are very keen for them to continue. They use them to recap on strategies for learning and to support next steps. They feel they are most useful in providing success criteria for every part of their learning, leading to steps for success. They like the freedom to make decisions about what they will record and how. They feel the mixture of teacher direction and their own reflection and recording is best.

OVER TO YOU

- Learning scrapbooks helped the children to become self-aware of their learning.

- How might you use this idea in your classroom?

- It might be useful to start with the learning walls and public prompts about heroes before moving to scrapbooks.

- When would you use scrapbooks — any time in the school day or at particular times?

- How might you structure your own learning scrapbook?

- What would be useful for the children to record?

- You could enable the children to interview everyday heroes about their learning strategies and how they use them in their everyday lives. Use scrapbooks to record notes and ideas.

- You might encourage the children to seek support and learning tips from their peers, adding Post-it® note comments about what they have noticed about their learning.

A MISCELLANY OF IDEAS

EMPATHY AND POOR BEHAVIOUR

We encourage children to stretch their empathy muscle when we are dealing with unfortunate incidents of poor behaviour. There are several pairs of old shoes in my office and I invite children to think about how their behaviour feels when in someone else's shoes by standing in them! The physical prompt can often help them to empathise more successfully. You can even swap shoes with the child and let them decide what they would do if they were the figure of authority.

SIGNS AROUND THE SCHOOL

Alongside all of the learning signs around the schools, how about quotes and phrases to imitate and inform learning-power conversations? A sign on our staffroom door informs, 'We may be sitting still but we are on a learning journey.' On the headteacher's door is 'Fear Not! Failure is the opportunity to begin again more intelligently.' The water cooler sports a Piaget quote, 'Intelligence is knowing what to do when you don't know what to do.' The library full of fiction has 'What is now proved was once only imagined.' (William Blake).

We make sure that we change the quotes every month or so to stimulate curiosity. Old signs quickly become merely wallpaper.

SHARING IDEAS WITH PARENTS

Next time you send a newsletter home suggest that parents ask their children not 'What have you done at school today?' but 'How have you learned at school today?' or 'What good questions did you ask at school today?' Offer parents some suggestions for follow-up questions. Encourage them to comment on 'hero stickers' that the children might be sporting as they leave school and ask 'Why are you Polly's hero today?' (See puppets, page 10) Another learning conversation started!

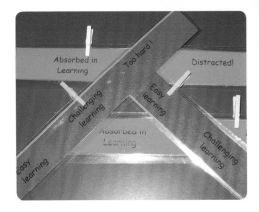

SINGING ABOUT LEARNING

Hero Raps

For the older children a great end to the week is the composition of a 'hero rap'. Using a simple beat and syllable pattern they can identify powerful learning heroes from the class and praise them in song! Use a song they think is cool as a template or make up a pattern of your own. Clapping, finger clicking and a certain amount of movement are almost obligatory!

PUPIL POWER

Chatter Trackers

Chatter trackers help put children in charge of their learning environment. A nominated pupil takes responsibility for indicating an acceptable level of noise in the classroom by moving a pointer to let the rest of the group know when the noise distraction is too high (or too low). A simple traffic light picture will do the trick. Apparently you can buy an electric noise monitor which flashes red above a certain level; but then a machine is taking charge instead of the children themselves managing distractions.

LEARNOMETERS / DISTRACTOMETERS...

Little ideas that reap huge benefits!

Little strips of laminated card and a peg can put children in charge of their learning a little more. Labelled 'Easy learning', 'Challenging learning' and 'Too hard' on one side, pupils use them to let you know whether you are meeting their learning needs or if they could do with more extension or support. It is powerful when learners realise that challenge is an essential element of their learning; that finishing easy tasks quickly does not signal cleverness but indicates time-filling rather than real learning.

The other side of this little strip is labelled 'Absorbed' at one end and 'Distracted' at the other. Teachers use this initially to help pupils monitor their absorption in learning but children will quickly begin to use it as a visual prompt to monitor themselves.

LEARNING HEROES IN THE CURRICULUM

In this section we find out how the idea of learning heroes has been incorporated into the curriculum, and the impact this has had on learning.

Firstly we see how the ideas have been put into practice in literacy, to improve story writing across the school or to develop children's imagination as they explore characterisation.

An ambitious outdoor project led by Kent's Outdoor Education Unit shows how the children's favourite learning heroes formed the basis of learning zones, collaborative challenges and maths problem-solving activities. The children were able to empathise with their learning heroes throughout the challenges and their confidence in maths has grown enormously.

Science too has been given the learning heroes treatment, and a cross-curricular project drew a wide range of subject areas together as children went about designing, making, writing and singing about their imaginary learning heroes.

Finally we are treated to a further selection of little ideas from across the curriculum, which help to grow children's awareness of their learning power.

IMPROVING STORY WRITING

WHERE WE STARTED

Our learning characters, Milan Reflective, Billy Resilient, Polly Reciprocity and Sylvie Resourceful, were used throughout the school to represent learning characteristics in a story. Our aim was to improve story-writing skills right across the school, in particular composition and effect; but also to deepen the children's understanding of learning capacities.

WHAT WE DID

A whole-school model story was written and adapted by class teachers to exemplify specific writing levels. The story introduced four characters and an unusual event which they experienced on the way home from school. The characters subsequently displayed very powerful learning behaviours during a science lesson the next day, e.g. sticking with a challenge instead of giving up, or using a range of resources to find information. The characters realised that they had become learning superheroes.

The classes learned the modelled story through pictures, words and actions.

If you don't know, ask!

HOW IT DEVELOPED

Once the children had absorbed the model story and language, they began to substitute other learning situations, e.g. planning and revising in DT, or learning by imitating an artist in art. They were demonstrating their knowledge and understanding of learning behaviours.

IMPACT ON THE CHILDREN

The story characters enabled the children to talk about their own positive and aspirational learning behaviours in a non-threatening way. 'Billy is good at persevering but he needs to ask for more challenging learning.' (Year 4 boy.) Gradually they began to talk about their own learning by referring back to the individual characters. 'I'm getting better at revising, just like Milan.' (Year 2 girl.) They could then consider how the characters might behave in a particular learning situation and use them as role models.

The children's story writing improved too. The regular modelling of the sequence, structure and language patterns in the story became so familiar to the children that they could reproduce the story verbally and with actions after a few retellings. They could arrange the pictures on the interactive whiteboard to recreate the story map and then write this story using the map and the actions as prompts. After a little time they began to adapt these stories, putting the characters in different learning situations and changing the story and the learning language accordingly. When sentence starters like 'frightened but curious' became 'furious but strangely calm' in a KS2 child's story we could be sure that children had learned about learning and could use and apply the literacy learning.

OVER TO YOU

Might you:

- Construct a model learning story around a character?
- Choose characters that appeal to your particular age group or school situation?
- Develop your own whole-school or class heroes to use in stories?
- Make story maps to get ideas going?
- Write sequels to the stories?
- Create hero books and add them to the library?
- Tell the stories to other classes or schools?
- Invite parents to read or hear the stories?

THE MODEL STORIES

Heroes Story Level 4

On a gloomy Autumn evening not very long ago four friends were walking home together. Their friendly chat was silenced when a circle of bright lights hovered above them. It then began to descend behind a clump of trees. Frightened but curious, the four friends walked towards the illuminous glow.

As they stood below the lights and looked up, a huge hatch opened. They heard a hypnotic hum while they were showered with tiny sparkling particles of dust. They wilted gently to the ground.

When they awake, the strange lights had disappeared. They wondered if it had been an illusion so decided to tell nobody and continued home.

The next day was science investigation day. Billy surprised himself by being really enthusiastic about the challenge and persevering even when the going got tough. He was not distracted by anything that happened around him but got lost in learning and creating a fantastic fair test.

Polly was dreading being in the same group as the 'good kids' but surprised herself by saying, "Okay, let's collaborate on this and we'll all learn better." She listened to the others in the group and thought about their points of view. The teacher was thrilled with the science learning of the whole group.

Sylvie lead her group of boys superbly. They asked great questions, found information from different sources and linked the facts together.

Milan did not rush in as usual but sat with his group, thought about what they needed to learn and planned how to do it. When their experiment started to go wrong he noticed immediately, helped the group to change the method and solved the problem. "You are a great learner," his friends praised.

They discussed their learning on the way home. "We have never learned like that before, it's like magic!" exclaimed Sylvie. Abruptly they stopped and looked at one another. "Do you think it has anything to do with the UFO?" murmured Milan. Four pairs of eyes opened wide. "We have been given super powers," whispered Billy. "We have become super-powerful learners! Yata!"

Heroes Story Level 2

One Autumn evening four friends were walking home from school. They were stunned into silence when they noticed a circle of bright lights descending from the sky. Frightened but curious, they walked towards the lights. As they stood beneath them sparkling dust fell on them and they began to feel very sleepy.

When they woke up the lights had gone so they thought they must have dreamed the whole thing.

The next day was science investigations. Billy felt excited about the challenge and did not give up when it got tricky, most unusual!

Polly listened to the others in her group and worked well as a team member, very unusual!

Sylvie helped her group to ask fantastic questions and use lots of resources to find the answers, highly unusual!

Milan planned carefully with his team, noticed when things needed to be changed and adapted the plan, unheard of!

Had the space dust given them learning power?

How could they use it?

WHERE WE STARTED

In Year 5 we wanted to focus primarily on developing resourcefulness with the children in Literacy. Using warm-ups, as described on page 13, resourceful learning capacities were introduced at the start of a lesson as part of the learning intention: for example, to make links between characters in different fables. The children began by exploring heroes, collecting pictures of their own role models and making notes about their own resourcefulness. As a class they created mobiles that celebrated and explained resourceful characteristics.

WHAT WE DID

Fables

The first unit explored was Fables. We use the integrated approach to Literacy and so follow the structure of reading, analysis, capturing ideas and writing. After reading a range of fables and identifying their organisational and language features, we invited the children to explore the characters and imagine what might happen if characters from different fables were to meet.

Using their imagination the children created new experiences for the tortoise and the hare. They were given questions to consider such as 'What might happen if the fox intercepted the hare?' The children collaborated to generate ideas, and decide which was the best.

Keeping within the characteristics previously identified, the children thought about how the characters might feel, what they might do, and what the outcome could be. They shared ideas, listened to each other and decided to create a role-play of their solution.

They then selected their best idea and planned the new fable using story maps. From this they built up the story from modelled, scribed, and supported to independent writing.

WHAT WE DID

Myths and Legends

Moving on from fables we encouraged the children to think about how Odysseus might have been resourceful. They thought about his qualities and skills using their knowledge of the character.

From this they designed their own mythical character, again with a focus on them being resourceful. Their new character was then to meet Odysseus; allowing the children to plan for a new myth.

IMPACT ON THE CHILDREN

The children's enthusiasm for learning has developed considerably. They are able to reflect on and apply resourceful learning behaviours in a range of contexts. This, in conjunction with the integrated teaching approach, has had a direct impac on the children's writing. Their fables and myths are imaginative and well planned; truly exploring character has allowed them to reflect on what they might do in different contexts.

The children are able to explain clearly how they are learning, and are developing an impressive range of strategies to help them move forward.

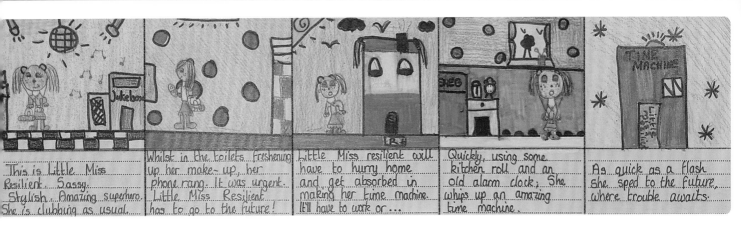

This is Little Miss Resilient. Sassy. Stylish. Amazing superhero. She is clubbing as usual.

Whilst in the toilets freshening up her make-up, her phone rang. It was urgent. Little Miss Resilient has to go to the future!

Little Miss resilient will have to hurry home and get absorbed in making her time machine. It'll have to work or ...

Quickly, using some kitchen roll and an old alarm clock, She whips up an amazing time machine.

As quick as a flash she sped to the future, where trouble awaits.

WHAT WE DID

Comics

Our work on learning heroes linked well with our book week where we were asking children to write in the style of a given author. We decided to explore the work of Roger Hargreaves and produce comics in the style of the Mr Men and Little Miss stories.

Whilst reading Mr Men stories we looked at extending the children's knowledge of characterisation through learning heroes. We considered what traits, skills and qualities Little Miss Reciprocity would have. Paired talk allowed children to delve deeper and decide how the characters might show their learning power in a range of contexts. We thought about settings, plot, and actions the character might take in each different element. This allowed for lots of powerful vocabulary development.

Using role play, hot-seating and telephone conversations with the characters we built a clearer picture of how the characters might behave. This in turn enabled the children to capture ideas for writing. We then used the Mr Men theme to create comics based on learning heroes. The children chose between Mr Resourceful and Miss Resilient.

IMPACT ON THE CHILDREN

The children were really excited about writing the comics and felt personally attached to the characters they had created. Strong understanding of characterisation enabled them to spend more time focusing on structure, organisation and layout, and developing the style of Roger Hargreaves. The quality of writing improved greatly as a result.

The children also have a greater understanding of the capacities: they can now recognise the learning behaviours they are using in everyday situations and identify improvements they need to make. They use the language of learning in their class discussions and describe themselves in these terms too.

OVER TO YOU

- How could you introduce learning heroes when planning a literacy unit?

- Which story characters exemplify learning capacities you have identified as needing development in your children?

- Could you invite real heroes into the school to develop, for example, newspaper reports?

- Could the children interview the hero using questions that explore their learning power?

- How about children writing biographies of famous learning heroes?

LEARNING HEROES IN MATHS

AN OUTDOOR MATHS CHALLENGE

WHERE WE STARTED

We were very lucky to be part of a learning-to-learn outdoors project led by Kent's Outdoor Education Unit. The project was supported by an Outdoor Education Adviser who worked closely with us to explore making the best use of our school grounds to develop learning-to-learn approaches linked to an area of the curriculum.

We wanted to create a maths trail to be used by children throughout the school to encourage teachers and children to make the best use of the outdoor learning environment. We were also keen to develop the children's knowledge and understanding of books, authors and characters and so decided to combine the two.

WHAT WE DID

Our Year 6 children carried out a survey to identify the children's favourite book characters throughout the school. The children wrote surveys and used frequency charts to record data. They then analysed the data using a range of bar charts and graphs and from these we selected the top five: *Harry Potter*, *Cinderella*, *Horrid Henry*, *Tracy Beaker* and *Captain Underpants*. These became our learning heroes, around which learning zones were defined within the school grounds. The children identified the four learning capacities each hero might use the most, and through their knowledge of the book began to identify how they used them. Within each zone the children were provided with a learning challenge that required collaborative learning. Once they had succeeded, the children had to add to their learning zone by creating maths problems.

HOW IT DEVELOPED

Harry Potter zone:

Harry Potter must cross the chess board to retrieve the Philosopher's stone, but there is a certain route he must follow and so must collaborate with others to cross the board. The children added coordinates to the board and set challenges where Harry had to cross obstacles at given points. Using his key learning capacities, the children devised strategies for overcoming the obstacles.

Activity:
Wizard's Chess (Card 2)
Rules (continued)
* You cannot walk around the chessboard.
* You cannot jump over squares.
* You can move backwards, forwards, left, right or diagonally.
* You must not use anything to mark the route as you go along.
* At the end, record the route in coordinates to receive bonus points.

Scoring
* Completing the route first time 10 points.
* Completing the route second time 5 points.
* Completing the route third time 3 points.
* Identifying the route in coordinates 5 points.

(Example on Card 3)

Activity:
Wizard's Chess (Card 1)
The Challenge
Find the route through the chessboard and get Harry, Ron and Hermione from one side to the other. Create a grid as set out below using cones or markers.

Rules
* Start on one side of the chessboard.
* Cross the chessboard by working out the correct route.
* As you enter a square you must identify its coordinates with your team mates.
* Only one person can be on the chessboard at any time.
* If you step into a wrong square you must go back to the start.

(Continued on Card 2)

Activity:
Wizard's Chess (Card 3)
Example
Here is one possible route. Now go and find yours.

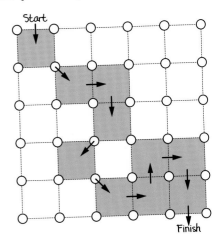

Tracy Beaker zone:

The home Tracy lives in has had a new security system installed. Tracy must escape without setting the alarm off. A simple spider web was constructed between two trees and the children had to find a way through without touching the web. Planning was of the utmost importance and the children soon found imitation and noticing to be extremely useful. The children decided to link this to mental calculation strategies, and created a diagram to match the web with a mental calculation for each part of the web. The calculations had to be solved correctly before moving through.

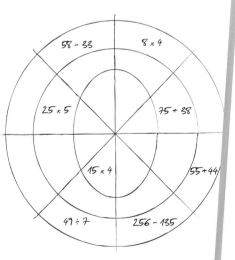

58 - 33	8 × 4
25 × 5	75 + 38
15 × 4	55 + 44
49 ÷ 7	256 - 135

Cinderella zone:

Cinderella and all her accomplices must be removed from the palace and get home before midnight. We used the trim trail equipment in our school grounds to support this. The children added to this by exploring time, using time equipment and measures.

Activity:
Cinderella's Obstacle Course

The Challenge
Cinderella and all her accomplices have to get home before the clock strikes midnight. However, there are lots of obstacles in the way that slow her down.

Rules
* All items must start at one end of the obstacle course.
* No items and no members of the group are allowed to touch the ground once they start on the course.
* If someone or something touches the ground they must return to the start.
* Nothing can be thrown.
* Everyone and everything must successfully travel to the end of the obstacle course.
* Use the stopwatch to time how long it takes to get the whole team and equipment from one end of the course to the other.
* Can you beat your time? Can you reorganise your team and equipment to make it quicker?
* Record your time in seconds, minutes and seconds and just minutes.

Horrid Henry zone:

Having raided Moody Margaret's camp, stolen all their pocket money and then dropped it all over the floor, the Purple Hand Gang, led by Horrid Henry must retrieve all the money.

Activity:
Horrid Henry's Raid

The Challenge
Horrid Henry must direct the Purple Hand Gang to each of the coins on the floor so they can pick them up and bring them to Henry. To stop Moody Margaret from getting the pocket money back Horrid Henry can only direct his gang using Horrid Henry's Top Secret Unbreakable Code..

Rules
* The Purple Hand Gang will all be blindfolded and cannot speak.
* The Purple Hand Gang can only walk slowly, hands out in front of them when directed by Horrid Henry.
* Horrid Henry cannot move and can only shout instructions.
* Horrid Henry can use names and the following code words only.

LEFT = TFEL	RIGHT = THGIR
GO = OG	STOP = POTS
PICK UP = PU KCIP	

Further challenges involved buying the maximum number of items with the money collected.

AN OUTDOOR MATHS CHALLENGE (CONTINUED)

Captain Underpants zone:

In the book Mr Krupp, the Headteacher, has confiscated Harold and George's latest copy of the comic 'Captain Underpants'. The boys must retrieve the comic without entering the Headteacher's office. Planning, revising, questioning and collaboration were used successfully. The children thought this was a good way to explore area and perimeter. They created a set of challenges which involved measuring accurately, calculating area and perimeter, and converting units.

George and Harold's Secret Mission (Card 2)

Hook a Comic

Equipment

- Rope
- Hook
- Bucket
- Table
- Chairs
- Questions Card

The Challenge

Using only the items around them George and Harold must retrieve the box containing the comic from the middle of the office.

The Rules

No one is allowed to enter the office as this will set off the alarm. You can only use the equipment found outside the office.

George and Harold's Secret Mission (Card 1)

The Scenario

Mr Krupp has taken George and Harold's latest copy of their comic "Captain Underpants" and locked it in his office. The boys must rescue the comic from the centre of his office without actually going into the room and setting off the security alarm.

The Challenge

Using only the items around them George and Harold must retrieve the box containing the comic from the middle of the office.

The Rules

No one is allowed to enter the office as this will set off the alarm. You can only use the equipment found outside the office.

George and Harold's Secret Mission (Card 3)

The problem

Mr Krupp would like to order some new office furniture but he's not sure how much space he has. Can you help?

- Measure the perimeter of the room,
- Measure the area of the room
- Using the furniture catalogue choose a new desk, chair and bookcase that would fit inside the room

Question 1

Mr Krupp measures a distance from his office door to his desk as 125 cm. How much is this in metres?

Question 2

Harold and George need to work out how much rope they need to hook the comic. Can you help by measuring the length and the width of the room in centimetres?

CAPTAIN UNDERPANTS

HOW IT PROGRESSED

Throughout the project we took lots of photographs of the children in action and created a photo-story film with motivational music. This had a big impact on the children because they could see how far they'd come and how using their learning power had helped them. We have continued to add to our challenges, both with the children and as a staff, adapting problems and challenges for different age groups.

IMPACT ON THE CHILDREN

Using learning heroes enabled the children to relate the learning capacities to contexts within a story and supported understanding of how they were used. The children empathised with the heroes throughout the challenges and so began to explore many learning skills. Their use of language changed following the learning challenges, and they were more confident in talking about how they learn in different contexts.

The children now find it easier to solve the maths problems because they are familiar with the heroes. They enjoyed writing and solving mathematical problems related to them and used learning language more effectively. Their confidence in Maths has grown enormously as they now fully appreciate that it's okay to make mistakes, imitate the processes used by others, and

be interdependent. The very practical nature of the project allowed the children to truly explore mathematical concepts and to question ideas and results. Having to have another go, to persevere in order to successfully complete challenges, made asking others for help okay.

The children's strategies for collaboration showed the most marked improvement, and using the film clip proved incredibly powerful in showing the children how they learn.

Children observed and commented on the following:

When we collaborate:

- It makes it a nice place to be — more pleasant
- It helps our friendships grow
- We're calmer, there's less stressing out
- We want to work WITH others
- We go with the flow and accept each other's ideas
- We get involved and focused on the task
- We support rather than blame each other
- We get things done more quickly
- We have more ideas
- We help people who are finding it tough
- We have trust.

OVER TO YOU

- Could you use famous or imaginary heroes to define learning zones in or around your school?

- How might you use heroes when introducing a maths topic?

- How about redesigning the classroom with your pupils — defining learning zones with heroes.

- How about creating imaginary hero characters and using them to develop maths problems that can be solved practically.

A RANGE OF IDEAS

Science with a Difference

Science is a subject area that fits seamlessly with the development of learning skills, particularly in developing the capacity to reason, imagine and make links.

Scientist Motivators

We assign certain scientists to particular science topic areas and use these scientists as motivators for the children's learning. We consider how the scientists had to relish a challenge, link knowledge together, see what pieces were missing and then use their imagination in deciding what the missing piece might be. Scientists have to be great planners and adapters and sometimes they work in partnership with other scientists or experts.

Teachers said things like 'What would Louis Pasteur have done when his experiment went wrong, would he have given up? Would he have changed it slightly?'

Teachers began to assess science learning in the voice of Charles Darwin when children had been categorising animals, or as Sir Isaac Newton during a topic on forces. Using a big picture of an appropriate scientific hero and a speech bubble the teachers appear around the classroom, comment on the children's learning so far and give hints or tips on how to move forward.

Empathy muscles were stretched by carrying out an investigation as if the children were Albert Einstein. Some crazy white wigs and white coats created atmosphere!

Detective Science...

Scientists have a lot in common with detectives. The children found out about some famous detectives or invented some detective characters of their own and then used these to help with science learning. They looked for clues and pieced them together in a scientific investigation. They had to interview others to get information and compare one account to another for anomalies. They were developing their questioning, distilling and reasoning skills the whole time.

Murder Mystery Science...

We start a science topic in a completely different way by inviting the pupils to a 'murder mystery party'. Characters are assigned to each member of the group in advance and they are asked to develop the role and wear a costume or carry a prop. Each character in the murder-mystery science lesson has a clue (or a red herring). They are interviewed by the investigator or gossip in corners to piece the picture together.

We take time after the lesson to discuss why we have chosen this way to begin learning a science topic. The children stretch their meta-learning muscles and explain how a scientist gathers information and makes discoveries piece by piece just as they did.

We challenge the children to use the greatest number of learning muscles during a science topic. They keep an account collectively as a whole class.

Visiting Scientists...

We found out from parents whether they use science in their jobs. We happened to have a dad who worked in forensics and he proved to be a super interviewee during Science Week. Equally valuable was input from a midwife mum, and an uncle who worked for a famous household cleaning-products company. The children asked them about their learning at school, how they used science in their jobs and whether they had to keep learning all of the time. School science suddenly became linked to real life and these family members were held in high esteem as learning heroes.

Imaginary Experiments...

The kinds of scientific investigation that pupils can carry out in school are limited to the safe and possible. Mr Fantastic from *The Fantastic Four* took his team up into space and accidentally caused them all to assume super powers by exposure to extremely high levels of radiation. He then worked tirelessly to find a way to turn 'The Thing' back into Ben Grim. Somewhat more exciting than growing a healthy broad bean plant.

We invited the children to design an imaginary experiment as if they were scientist superheroes. In imagining the scenario and the problem, hypothesising about the solution, and designing an experiment to test their theory, pupils were using all of the same learning skills but in a much more heroic imaginary situation. This was a wonderful challenge for our more able pupils.

OVER TO YOU

- Could each of your classes 'adopt' a famous scientist as a learning hero? The beginning lessons of the school year could focus on a class biography of the chosen hero.

- Might you assign an appropriate scientist to strands of science learning, e.g. Sir Isaac Newton and forces, and use them to motivate and nudge the children's learning behaviours.

- How about adding a bit of humour to science lessons with an old deerstalker and a pipe, or a policemen's helmet and a notebook, to costume your scientific investigators?

- Have you any real-life scientists in your school or local community who could help to anchor your pupils' learning in everyday life?

- Do you have a school website or a virtual learning platform where young science heroes could set challenges for one another?

- How about a giant test tube display that fills up as the children stick on Post-its® of learning muscles stretched during a science topic. Different colours for the 4 R's might be good too.

A CROSS-CURRICULAR PROJECT

WHERE WE STARTED

Our exploration of learning heroes with our Year 6 children had been so successful that we decided to undertake a cross-curricular project based around imaginary heroes. The children would create a set of imaginary heroes in order to share their understanding and use of learning power with younger children in the school. We hoped this would give a deeper understanding, and hence use, of learning capacities — going beyond the language to practical use.

WHAT WE DID

The project allowed us to explore many areas of the curriculum to develop and extend the children's learning. In Literacy we read, analysed and created job descriptions and newspaper reports about learning heroes. We used hot-seating to empathise with heroes and created freeze-frames of possible scenarios. Planned progression included creating 3D models of the heroes using design technology skills; and carrying out focused practical tasks based around materials and structures, leading on to design and make challenges. This incorporated practical use of measures in numeracy. Use of a range of media and study of texture integrated into art and design. The children were keen to develop jingles for advertising their heroes, using slogans and catchphrases.

HOW IT DEVELOPED

One group decided to create a hero to support the many EAL children in the school. What really impressed us here were the learning capacities they chose as vital strengths; imitation, collaboration, listening, noticing, absorption and making links.

Another group created a hero to help Year 3 children become better learners. They selected blinkers as the hero's prop: she was always focused and looking forward.

LEARNING HERO WANTED!

MUST BE ABLE TO:
- COLLABORATE WITH MAY DIFFERENT TYPES OF PEOPLE
- GET ABSORBED IN ANY TYPE OF WORK/ACTIVITY
- NOTICE GOOD THINGS AROUND THEM
- MANAGE ALL OF THEIR DISTRACTIONS
- REASON WHY THEY SHOULD DO SOMETHING, NOT JUST DO IT FOR THE SAKE OF DOING IT
- IMAGINE WHAT SOMETHING WOULD BE LIKE AS THE FINISHED ARTICLE

They used the catchphrase 'Try, try and you WILL fly' as a motivator. They felt this hero would need to help Year 3 children with planning and imitation, so they created games to exercise these learning capacities. For example, they created simple mirroring games where children had to imitate the movements of others. After the game they talked about how they had imitated their partner, and gave examples of where and how they could use the learning capacities to become better learners.

IMPACT ON THE CHILDREN

The Year 6 pupils were pleased to be 'the experts', sharing their learning with younger children. The younger children too found it exciting to learn from older children. They listened intently and readily joined in the activities.

Multi-media presentations of heroes

Use PowerPoint to create a presentation

Investigate models of toy heroes

Design and make an imaginary learning hero

Design:
1. sketch ideas
2. select
3. annotated drawing
4. design spec.
5. plan, make
6. evaluate

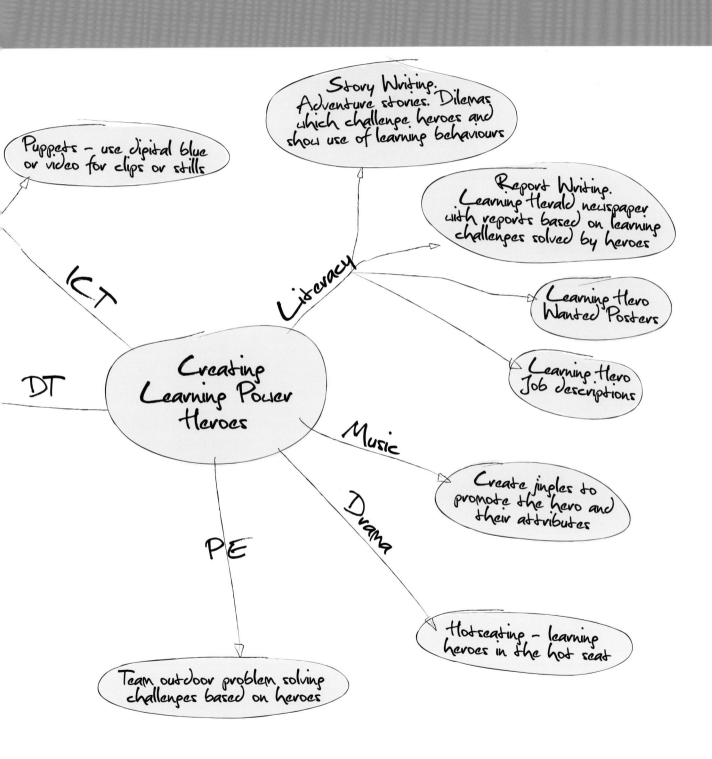

Story Writing.
Adventure stories. Dilemas which challenge heroes and show use of learning behaviours

Puppets - use digital blue or video for clips or stills

Report Writing.
Learning Herald newspaper with reports based on learning challenges solved by heroes

Learning Hero Wanted Posters

ICT

Literacy

Learning Hero Job descriptions

DT

Creating Learning Power Heroes

Music

Create jingles to promote the hero and their attributes

Drama

PE

Hotseating - learning heroes in the hot seat

Team outdoor problem solving challenges based on heroes

A MISCELLANY OF IDEAS

Daemons

In his books *Northern Lights* and *The Golden Compass* Philip Pullman gives every human a 'daemon'. It is like a soul or a conscience outside their body. We invited older pupils to decide what animal their 'learning daemon' would be and to try to imagine it commenting on their learning. They were encouraged to think of choosing something that helped them reach a target: e.g. a tiger has great focus when hunting and is not distracted from the task by anything.

Physical Education

The PE curriculum has a section on 'Outdoor Adventurous Activities'. Do you have a space in school where you could set up a simple obstacle course with a rope guide? Night lining is a great way to really highlight the elements of reciprocity and clear communication.

The group of pupils all don a blindfold except for the leader, and are led to the obstacle course. The object of the exercise is that they all hold onto one another and the leader has to pass back instructions to get the team around the obstacle course. They must find a way to ensure that they all understand the instructions and that the line does not get broken so that no members can get lost. There has to be excellent collaboration and empathy, the leader must notice details and find the best way of sharing the information, and of course the team must be willing to ask questions.

At the end of the exercise it is interesting to ask the group to make a list of all the learning muscles they think they used in the activity.

ICT

We used the 'creating multi-media presentations' part of the curriculum to make stop-frame animation stories of learning. Little plasticine characters had learning dilemmas or revelations that helped them to progress as learners.

Making animations meant that the children were collaborating, planning, revising, imitating… a host of BLP capacities as they put the film together. Writing the screenplay and the script had them talking 'learnish' to one another in order to perfect the story line.

The films were shared with other classes, groups, and even parents, and turned into a family learning experience.

Of course there could be more independence involved. The pupils could decide what kind of film to make… a documentary, a docu-drama, a learning promotion film in the style of a music video. Why not make a really big deal of the end results and have a premiere?

Robot Wars...

love to see the family teams on Robot Wars nd am impressed by the amount of science nd technology learning these teams have aced together. With some neighbouring chools we have decided to give our own ersion of Robot Wars a go next term.

We will challenge the learning amilies to design a moving vehicle o undertake a number of tests.

- Uniqueness of design; no restrictions.

- Longest distance when rolled down a ramp; length of ramp, angle and surface to be given in advance.

- Greatest resilience when hit by a swinging football 3 times; how many bits drop off!

- How many learning muscles stretched by the projects; list and examples required.

he families and vehicles will meet t a designated time and place hen... 'Let the wars begin!'

A Learned List

We invited the children to make themselves a 'Things I have Learned in my Life' scroll or book. They were to get as much help as they could from friends and family in order to make the most comprehensive list they could. We gave them time to share their lists with one another so that one idea inspired another until they felt their list was as complete as it could be. Each time they learn something new, in or out of school, they add it to their list. It has proved be a super weekly celebration to hear about and congratulate additions.

'My son would this week add "How to yo-yo". It took a great deal of perseverance and imitation of his uncle Graeme, and deserves praise as much as any NC learning intention.'

OVER TO YOU

How about getting parents, families and visitors involved and using up some of that old printer paper that comes as a great long folded strip, or an old fax paper roll.

A class could be designated as 'Keepers of the List' to make sure there are no duplications, but anyone who comes to the school could be offered the opportunity to add learning to the list.

LEARNED LIST

* How to trot on a horse
  Jane

* How to ride a pedalo
  Connor W

* Ride my bike without using stabilisers
  Phoebe

* To swim!   Emily P

* To dive!   Finn

* How to cannonball jump into the water
  William C

* Put my face in the water and blow bubbles
  Joseph H

* How to say 'strawberries and cream' in Dutch
  Mrs Brandon

* How to steer a boat
  Laura and Sarah G

* How to play table tennis
  Ben

* How to hold a frog!
  Georgia H

* Make fresh apple juice!
  Mrs Day

* That Pluto is not classified as a planet anymore.
  Faith

TRANSFORMING LEARNING

Learning Hero Headteachers
- Nayland Primary School, Suffolk
- Christ Church C of E Primary School, Folkestone

Learning Hero Teachers
- Year 6 Teacher,
  Christ Church C of E Primary School
- Year 6 Teacher,
  Christ Church C of E Primary School
- Reception Teacher,
  Nayland Primary School

Pupils as Learning Heroes
- Year 2 Pupil,
  Bures Primary School
- Year 4 Pupil,
  Nayland Primary School
- Year 6 Pupil,
  Christ Church C of E Primary School
- Year 6 Pupil,
  Christ Church C of E Primary School

LEARNING HEROES WHO TRANSFORM LEARNING

Within the pages of this book we have been treated to inspiring accounts of rich learning environments. These environments represent a transformation in learning and teaching, and certainly don't come about unaided.

Transforming learning throughout a school is a significant and worthwhile undertaking by the head teacher, teachers, learning assistants, and of course the children themselves. The path can be joyful, challenging, inspirational and downright difficult.

In this section we hear from two of the head teachers of the featured schools. Their accounts give a flavour of the passion, dedication and sheer hard work involved in taking the philosophy and practice of learning power forward.

Teachers too have to make an effort to change their practice, often moving from over-supporting or spoon-feeding children to acting as a learning coach. The teachers' accounts show a variety of initial concerns, how these were overcome, and how they now relish their new role.

And children have to change their relationships with their teachers. They may resist having to think for themselves, or find the answers; it's easier to stay dependent! But fortunately their teachers persevered and now the children enjoy their new-found independence and love of learning.

LEARNING HERO HEADTEACHERS

RAEGAN DELANEY
Headteacher, Nayland
Primary School

Finding a Prince

'You have to kiss a lot of frogs before you find your prince' and that is pretty much how I feel about conferences, head teacher meetings and INSET courses after so many years in education. But when a young teacher from Bath told a children's philosophy story about learning, and a group of head teachers talked about Building Learning Power at an NCSL event in Autumn 2005, they caught my attention just enough for me to get on the internet and order the *Building Learning Power* book.

Guy Claxton's book struck a number of chords with me, and his talk of bagpipe-playing head teachers and life-long learning skills inspired me enough to make BLP an agenda item at the next steering group meeting for our learning partnership. Here it caught the interest of primary, middle and upper school senior leaders, and we agreed to send a delegation to Bath to visit some of the schools, and most importantly talk to some of the pupils.

In a small open-plan Year 4 classroom in Bath, I met Aaron who made me realise why BLP wasn't just interesting, but was necessary for the children in my school, our partnership and ultimately beyond. Here's part of the conversation…

Me: *So, there are displays all around your school about Building Learning Power, what's all that about?*

Him: *Are you a teacher?*

Me: *Yes.*

Him: (Deep sigh, raise eyes skywards) *Ok, imagine my teacher is over there at the front teaching a fantastic science lesson. She's got apparatus and everything and is teaching us something great and really important.*

Me: *Ok.*

Him: *And there's a boy over there messing about, doing something a bit stupid but funny. I am watching him and not the teacher. It doesn't matter how great her teaching is I have not learned anything because I have not learned how to manage my distractions.*

After all those frogs I had finally found my prince!

Spreading the News

I returned to my own school and learning community absolutely bubbling over with enthusiasm and remembering why I had become a teacher in the first place. While our learning partnership planned formal training for senior leaders and a mix of teachers and learning support assistants, I read everything I could on BLP and began trying

things out with classes whenever I taught.

A day dedicated to BLP for senior leaders from our partnership was crucial. If the scho leaders believe in learning to learn and put it high on the school development agenda, the it can impact on the whole school. When the leaders of the first, middle and upper schools in a pyramid sign up to BLP then you are creating the possibility of nursery childre in a learning environment that will continue to upper sixth, and that is truly exciting. Ultimately the upper school has everything to gain: imagine teaching these hungry, independent learners from my nursery class when they reach GCSE and A level!

Training and Development

With a Nayland Year 4 teacher and TA involved in training and action research in one class, and myself constantly drip feeding children and staff about BLP, the rest of the team was determined not to wait. We held whole-staff training and agreed not to get caught up in the minutiae but to share the big picture of learning with our children and families. BLP has evolved and threaded itself into the fibre of our school.

There have been lots of questions and development ideas since then: how to includ BLP on our planning (we add the learning-power capacity we have in mind to the end of the learning intention in purple print because purple was the colour of power in ancient Rome!): how to incorporate BLP into our story-making ideas and assemblies; and lots of other brainwaves that we have shared in this book. Mostly we keep our eye on the learning ball and make sure that everything we do is focused on children's learning.

My Job

My job is to ask the questions and make the comments that keep BLP fresh for children, families and staff. Noticing the new ideas that appear in the learning of one class and encouraging imitation by others, encouraging parent to add their learning to the boaster oster board, accepting the challenge of o-authoring a book, and sharing my fears nd perseverance with the other learners in ur community — being the head learner!

When I was showing a local AST around chool a few weeks ago, our Year 4 teacher aid she didn't really do much about BLP nese days and later came to apologise if he had said the wrong thing. She hadn't, totally understand what she meant. The hildren's learning, her teaching and the lassroom environment are drenched in BLP ut, along with the rest of Nayland School, t is no longer something that we 'do', it has become part of what we *are*.

JIM KREISELMEIER

Headteacher, Christ Church C of E Primary School

Why BLP?

Building Learning Power supports a holistic approach to learning where everyone is successful; it breaks down stereotypes about learning and challenges thinking about how we best ensure that our earners develop. It considers everyone as a learner, recognises that learning is portable, and identifies strategies we can use to make learning more effective.

BLP helps teachers and teaching assistants to help children to learn how to learn, in the classroom and in the community. My core belief in education is that learning takes place within all aspects of community ife. We have invested much time and enthusiasm in developing study support, providing opportunities for learning outside of the classroom. We had to think carefully about how we could capture children's attention and imagination to make them want to attend. The training we have provided has supported these

aims to ensure that all our staff share the same perspective about learning and see the value it adds out of school hours.

How we went about it

I've trained nine cohorts, each of between four and eight members of staff. We decided to have a mixture of teachers and support staff in each group to blur the boundaries of who the teacher is. I firmly believe that everyone that works with children is responsible for teaching and learning and has an impact on children's learning. We've built strong relationships this way as everyone is involved. We challenged the notion of 'super head' or 'super teacher' because it's about team work. That's why BLP is so fundamental to the educational strategy of our school.

We've been developing our creative curriculum, which includes key skills and

a sharp focus on literacy and numeracy, but BLP underpins it all: it is central to personalising learning for children.

We've used learning heroes in history and science, and the children have also identified heroes amongst their peers and members of staff. This has helped deepen understanding and has supported children who needed support and engagement.

Where are we now?

We've just completed more training and some teachers have really embedded learning power into their everyday practice. We have a staff training day at the end of each term in school, preparing a practical activity to develop BLP skills. We ensure learning power is a regular feature of all staff and team meetings and discussions.

Where next?

We need to ensure BLP is planned for at the medium- and short-term planning stages. We'd like to develop the dual learning intention approach; making clear which muscle we're flexing in every lesson.

It's about sustainability now, keeping BLP on the agenda and taking a fresh look at regular intervals. Support and guidance are crucial to ensure progression and the message is clear that this is what we're about.

I have found it useful to refer to a TLO resource: *The Learning Focused School — A Self-Reflection Tool* as I feel it is practical and simple guidance for helping BLP to become a reality in classrooms. It needs dedicated professional development for all the staff and a continual refreshing of ideas.

TRANSFORMING LEARNING

LEARNING HERO TEACHERS

SARAH MERRITT

Year 6 Teacher and KS2
Team Leader, Christ Church
C of E Primary School

I couldn't imagine teaching without BLP now. My children understand how to develop as learners; they don't need me as much as they thought they did. They're aware of what they need to do and how, and therefore are more in control of what they do next.

Children Take It On

To begin with I was concerned about how children from our part of Folkestone could understand the language and the processes and use them. But they do, and I have been delighted with how readily they have taken new ideas and strategies on board to develop their way forward. BLP has had a real impact on all areas of the curriculum; the children are aware of how they're learning all of the time, in everything they do.

Going Deeper

When we started two years ago we looked carefully at the children and decided what they needed most. The children needed to build their collaboration skills. This year they had this but were very passive: they sat back and waited for things to happen; the classic good student versus good learner. So they needed to develop strategies for being more resourceful learners. We found we really needed to get underneath each learning capacity, breaking it down into success criteria.

For example when considering how to collaborate effectively with others the children list the small steps and processes needed.

Initially their suggestions were quite broad, e.g. 'team work', but as time went on and understanding developed through deeper questioning and asking the children 'how' at each stage, their success criteria grew. They might now include listening, sharing ideas, watching, agreeing a leader and making sure everyone is involved.

Using Heroes

We've used learning heroes this year because we needed to make learning to learn more explicit. We used a cross-curricular approach and began by introducing heroes linked to the curriculum. As confidence grew the children selected heroes from a wide range of contexts.

My Development

BLP has really helped me develop my approach to teaching and learning. I have become very good at helping the children to identify success criteria, drawing out the small steps they need to remember. We have dual learning intentions which identify both what we need to do and how. I like to analyse how the children have been learning in the plenary, to help them evaluate what went well, what didn't, and why.

A Change in Role

I like to leave the children to consider their success. If a lesson is not working I'll let them fail and then discuss how and why. For example we play 'target number' as a warm-up. The children have to find as many ways of achieving the target as possible. Some children made lots of errors at the beginning of the year, either through using symbols incorrectly or miscalculating. Through class discussion and children modelling methods and ideas on the interactive whiteboard, they have learnt to imitate each other's approaches. I give less instruction, and more time for them to reflect. The children are more able to do this and can say why and how things went wrong without feeling worried about it.

I do less directed teaching. I will use learning-to-learn and let the children find the way, because I'm confident they understand how to use their learning-power capacities, and now I do too!

Next year we'll analyse the children and then decide what we need to do and how. We'll definitely use learning heroes; it made learning come alive for the children.

RITCHIE HULKS

Year 6 Teacher and Creative Curriculum Leader, Christ Church C of E Primary School

Getting Started

I was first introduced to BLP three and half years ago when I was a teaching assistant at the school in Year 2. I have to admit I was a bit sceptical at first; I thought it was the next new initiative and was concerned about fitting everything in, that it would be great for a term and then it'd be forgotten.

I developed a challenge corner which focused on trying to get the children to think about their surroundings. This actually had very little to do with learning how to learn, which was a lack of understanding on my part at the time. I then moved into Year 1 to do my graduate teacher programme. We developed a learning wall which aimed to maintain the focus with the children. We had a kite with the four R's on the tail and we used a class learning journal which we filled in at the end of each day. We focused on developing the language, using stuck strategies, and looking for clues to help us learn.

Going Deeper

When I moved into Year 6 in 2006 I experienced a big change. Rather than thinking of BLP as the four dispositions we went into the learning capacities. We focused on developing the children's collaboration. Having discussed with colleagues we decided that collaboration would be the learning capacity that would have the biggest impact.

This year we wanted to do something different to keep it fresh and not stand still. The first couple of weeks in September are key; we just observe the children and question them about their learning. This year they were very needy; they lacked independence. When we talked to them

about BLP they knew the words but they didn't know what they meant and couldn't demonstrate how to use them, so we focused on people who could — learning heroes.

We used famous heroes to model learning behaviours and then developed a range of *'warming up for learning'* sessions to allow the children to identify and practise using strategies for them. For example, when we were warming up our noticing skills in Literacy we provided the children with a range of photographs of the Blitz during World War II; We were working through a narrative writing unit and were at the *'capturing ideas'* stage, so we wanted the children to notice details about the impact of the bombs on the buildings and people. Having listed strategies for effective noticing, such as looking closely at the obvious and the not so obvious, talking to a partner about ideas, questioning ideas and thoughts, we gave the children five

minutes to see what they could notice about the impact of the bombs. Noticing skills were then used in the main part of the lesson to improve sentences written about the pictures.

Still Learning

I still have to think about which learning capacity to use how and when, it's certainly not automatic. I have to make sure I make them explicit all the time and plan in when we're going to use what. It's important to keep BLP at the forefront of what you do.

The Children

BLP has made making an impact on children's attitudes to learning easier. It has made the children realise that school isn't just about reading, writing and maths; it's about how you learn and what sort of person you are too! Using specific learning heroes to support certain children has enabled them to see beyond barriers they previously had. BLP has helped to make our children become more independent as learners.

LEARNING HERO TEACHERS

GINNY DAY
Reception Teacher, Nayland Primary School

How it Started

When the head teacher returned from a conference in London with 'that look' there was a deep intake of breath at Nayland School: 'What now?' The 'what' was Building Learning Power and over the next couple of months we all became enthused by this framework, and even more so by the central message — that children should always know what they are learning, but equally how they learn.

A Fit with Foundation Stage

As a teacher in the Foundation Stage the presumption might be that my children are too young to cope with the language and the concept of learning to learn. I totally disagree with this perception. At Nayland School we have a complete belief in, and commitment to, the importance of the foundations of learning. We have a set of sayings from a long forgotten source, *'foundations take longer to create than buildings; the higher the building the firmer the foundations need to be and if foundations prove inadequate it is very, very expensive, if indeed possible, to underpin them later on.'* From this ethos we decided that BLP had to go from the youngest children up and not be used as an extra in the later years of school.

What We Do

The planning was all about how to present the learning capacities and the language to children verbally, visually and in a concrete way. You can see the displays, the puppets and toolboxes in this book. What you cannot see is the constant drip feed of the learning language, the teachers' commentary which nudges the children's learning behaviours along, and the way that these very young children pick up on this modelled language and understand what it means when they use it themselves.

Children's Understanding

When a five-year-old who is struggling with a jigsaw puzzle doesn't give up but asks for a collaborator and explains that they are enjoying the challenge, or an adult who is struggling is presented with the 'hammer of perseverance', then you know that these children are gaining skills that will stay with them for the rest of their lives.

The six areas of learning, with PSE at the centre, marry up perfectly with BLP. The new EYFS curriculum focusing on the unique child and personalised learning fit so well with the underlying principles of BLP. After two years I can see as I plan the learning opportunities for my children which learning-power muscle will be strengthened as we learn. What's more the children often tell me before I even get there. It has become less of a way of doing things and more of **a way of being**.

As an early years teacher, the question is not whether you can use BLP, but how can you possibly not!

PUPILS AS LEARNING HEROES

DEVELOPING INDEPENDENCE

Our Year 6 children struggled to build their learning power effectively to begin with. This was partly due to a lack of understanding of the learning capacities and how to use them, but also because the children were used to listening and responding rather than finding their own way. They found it difficult to answer our 'but why?' and 'but how?' questions initially. However, we persevered and as the children began to see that finding out for themselves was fun their enthusiasm increased. Using learning heroes helped a great deal. We played a murder mystery game right at the start using heroes the children had come up with for homelearning. They enjoyed seeing their heroes in a different situation but were able to use their knowledge and understanding of them to solve the problem. This in turn made it easy to open conversations about their own learning as they made links with heroes they knew and situations they had been in.

Our children have gone from strength to strength and now talk confidently about how they are learning, what they do well and what they need to work on. Relationships with peers and adults have developed well and we feel this will particularly support the children in their transition to secondary school.

LUCAS
Year 2, Bures Primary School

"Powerful learners never give up. When I was skiing at first I found it really hard to learn my snow plough but I didn't give up and I was able to do it. Powerful learners like a challenge like learning how to ride down a hill on your bike without crashing at the bottom. When I had my first horse riding lesson I had to keep an eye on my horse and notice what he was doing because he was quite young, I imitated my mum when I learned how to trot.

You can be a great learner all of the time, I'm a powerful learner in school too!"

DANIELLE
Year 4, Nayland Primary

"Building Learning Power is fun and is a great way of helping children to learn. I learnt new words like reciprocity and reflectiveness, but I especially liked the made up words like 'Learnatic' 'Head learner' and 'Brainiac'. It encouraged my class to work as a team and produce some great pieces of work whilst having FUN at the same time. We have building learning power everywhere in Nayland School!"

KAYLEIGH
Year 6, Christ Church C of E

"Yes, building our learning power definitely brought people together more in our class. I like to be doing rather than listening and BLP has made me do more. You can choose your own and even make your own; it's more fun when we have our say. I liked using Father Christmas, it was funny.

When you have famous heroes it makes it exciting because you want to know what they're like. When we meet the heroes we can definitely be sure they're really like that and Mrs Merritt isn't just making it up. It's good to know people from around the school and find out what they do and how."

ILIR
Year 6, Christ Church C of E

"I've learned words I never knew before. I liked starting with Michael Owen because I like him as a footballer. It helped me just think of what he did and to never give up. Cesc Fabrigas would be my ultimate hero because I support Arsenal and he shows real resilience — he perseveres. He also collaborates well with his team mates and plans his moves.

Mrs Merritt would make a good hero; she makes links by joining people's ideas together, she's always totally absorbed in what she's doing — like today in dance when she wouldn't think about anything but. She includes everyone and tries to make learning happy and enjoyable so she thinks about how we're feeling, she empathises. She tries her hardest and makes it fun for everyone, she varies it and shows us lots of ways of doing the same thing."

FURTHER READING

Building Learning Power
by *Guy Claxton*

International research into how the mind works shows that we are all capable of becoming better learners. *Building Learning Power* applies this research directly to the work of teachers in classrooms, to provide a practical framework for fostering lifelong learning in all young people.

What's the Point of School?
by *Guy Claxton (Oneworld Publishing)*

Education's key responsibility should be to create enthusiastic learners who will go on to thrive in a swiftly changing world. Written with passion, wit, and authority this book blends practical examples with the latest advances in brain science and will inspire teachers and parents to foster a natural curiosity and spirit of adventure in the next generation.

Building 101 Ways to Learning Power
by *Maryl Chambers, Graham Powell* and *Guy Claxton*

For teachers starting to explore learning power in their classrooms: this handbook encourages you to think that bit differently about how you can engage with your students in helping them to become better learners.

Learning to Learn — The Fourth Generation
by *Guy Claxton*

How do children learn? Can they be helped to do it better? If so, what is involved? And is 'learning to learn' an accessory to the core business of schools, a distraction from it, or a new way of thinking about what that core business is?

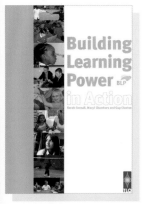

Building Learning Power in Action
by *Sarah Gornall, Maryl Chambers* and *Guy Claxton*

Building Learning Power in Action shows how some schools have embraced BLP, and captures the exciting effects it is having in classrooms. It describes a range of real live examples where busy teachers have tried out some aspects of BLP, and been (to put it mildly) pleasantly surprised by the results.

Pathways to Coaching
by *Graham Powell, Maryl Chambers* and *Gillian Baxter*

This handbook explains the what, why and how of coaching. It explores the skills that will enable team leaders to put coaching into practice with their team.

Training and consultancy

TLO Limited provide a range of training opportunities to support Building Learning Power.

To find out more, visit:
buildinglearningpower.co.uk

Or contact:

TLO Limited
Henleaze House
Harbury Road
Bristol
BS9 4PN

t: 0117 **989 8204**

f: 0117 **907 7897**

e: **office@tloltd.co.uk**

TLO

Professor Guy Claxton is programme consultant, and chief inspiration, for the Building Learning Power programme.

PHOTO CREDITS

The following images reproduced under Creative Commons Attribution, Attribution-NoDerivs or Attribution-ShareAlike licence: conditions as at http://creativecommons.org/licences

page 12: Santa
http://www.flickr.com/photos/
snapeverything/3121885093/

page 12: Charlie Bucket
http://www.flickr.com/photos/
the_wb/2764719340/

page 15: Nelson Mandela
http://www.flickr.com/photos/
32912172@N00/2681406879/

page 21: Jigsaw Puzzle
http://www.flickr.com/photos/
jemsweb/19976952/sizes/o/

page 30: Sharing Ideas With Parents
http://www.flickr.com/photos/
ranoush/2842954913/

page 39: Cinderella
http://www.flickr.com/photos/
edenpictures/2994064840/

page 39: Horrid Henry
http://www.flickr.com/photos/
ciamabue/2686465176/

page 40: Captain Underpants
http://www.flickr.com/photos/
cesarastudillo/2808676292/

page 42: Detective Science
http://www.flickr.com/photos/
oddharmonic/2525129589/

page 42: Murder Mystery Science
http://www.flickr.com/photos/
miikkah/885943722/

page 43: Visiting Scientists
http://www.flickr.com/photos/
sanjoselibrary/2968368894/

page 43: Imaginary Experiments
http://www.flickr.com/photos/
futureshape/3104642948/

page 44: Cowboy
http://www.flickr.com/photos/
klobetime/416694616/

page 46: Daemon
http://www.flickr.com/photos/
brook/27793774/

page 46: Obstacle Course
http://www.flickr.com/photos/
alecea/2557741745/

page 46: ICT
http://www.flickr.com/photos/
danielpaquet/438161195/

page 47: Robot Wars
http://www.flickr.com/photos/
uriel1998/2988340736/

page 47: Learned List
http://www.flickr.com/photos/
62337512@N00/2615993927/

IMAGE CREDIT

page 39: "Tracy Beaker"
by Brian Davies, 2009